GW01377283

Written by Dominique Joly
Illustrated by Jean-Claude Senée

*Specialist adviser:
Sarah Heath,
M. Phil Conservation Policy*

*ISBN 1 85103 160 X
First published 1992 in the United Kingdom
by Moonlight Publishing Ltd,
36 Stratford Road, London W8
Translated by Jane Churchill*

*© 1988 by Gallimard Jeunesse
English Text © 1992 by Moonlight Publishing Ltd
Printed in Italy by Editoriale Libraria*

POCKET • WORLDS

Farm Animals Around the World

The animals you see on farms today have wild ancestors...

THE ANIMAL WORLD

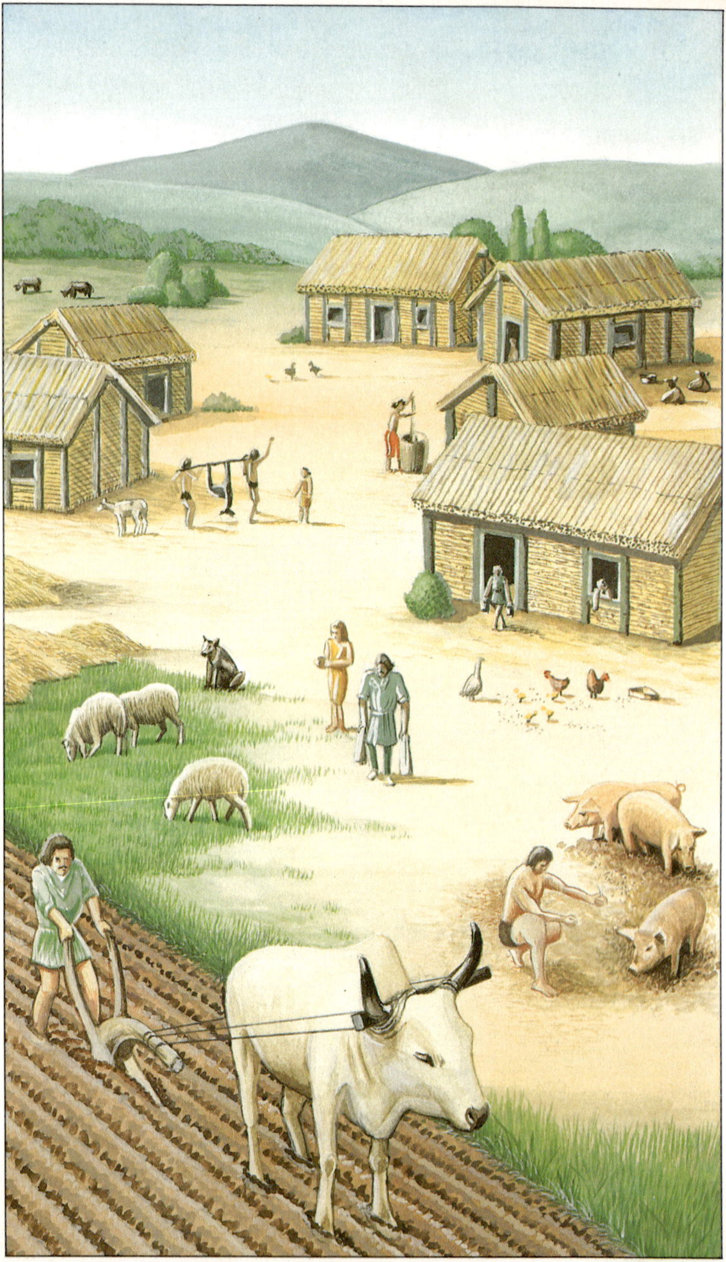

Long ago, people had to hunt for their food. But over the centuries, they learnt how to tame and keep herds of cattle, sheep and goats. Villages began to grow.

The cow's ancestor, the aurochs, was strong and probably very fierce.

The animals provided a steady supply of fresh meat. Their skins were used for clothing. Oxen and horses carried loads and also helped farmers cultivate their land. **They had become domesticated.**
Little by little the animals changed. Farmers found out they could cross different breeds. This meant they could rear sheep with extra-thick fleeces for their wool or dairy cows that produced more milk.

Wild boars and wild sheep are the ancestors of pigs and sheep.

In this traditional farmyard, chickens and ducks scratch about freely. You might also see rabbits, which in Europe are bred for their meat.

The cock rules the roost, rabbits live in hutches, pigs in sties and ducks enjoy a paddle in the pond.

A farm is made up of several different buildings.

They may be scattered about the fields, or grouped around the farmyard. Everyone needs a home: shelters for all the animals, sheds for the farm machinery, barns for storing hay and straw and, of course, a farmhouse for the farmer and his family!

Nearby, there is sometimes a kitchen garden where the farmer grows vegetables: further away stretch meadows and fields of crops to feed both people and animals.

When the nights grow cold in winter, the cows are brought in to their cowsheds.

In a flock of sheep, one ram fathers many lambs. You can recognise him by his curly horns.

What a hullaballoo in the farmyard!
It's feeding time. Geese crane their necks, guinea fowl shriek, and chickens run about clucking and squawking.

Can you spot the turkey strutting about, a cock and his hen fussing around their chicks, and a duck with her ducklings?

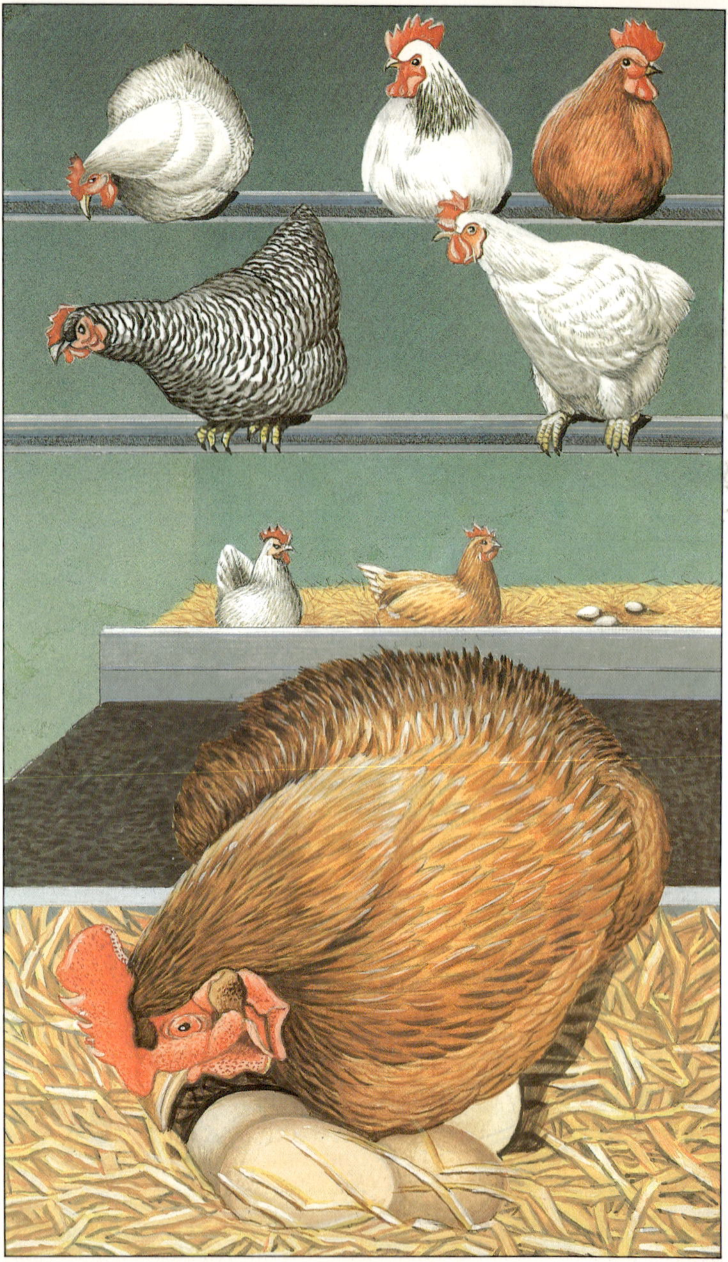

Hens do not like being disturbed in their cosy hen-house.

When it is dark, they flutter onto their perches, to sleep. The birds who roost on the highest ones are the leaders of the flock. They make the rules and peck any chicken lower down who misbehaves! This is where the expression 'the pecking order' comes from.

When laying an egg, a hens puffs out her feathers and clucks loudly.
A broody hen will sit on her eggs to keep them warm. If the eggs have been fertilized by the cock, her chicks will hatch out in 21 days.

Chickens hate water! To clean themselves, they take dust baths. They crouch down, ruffle their feathers and shake the dust over themselves.

Ducks preen their feathers regularly to keep them waterproof.

What do you think the duck is doing with its tail in the air? It is looking for insects, leaves and grasses to eat. Have you watched ducks using their webbed feet to swim?

Guinea fowl are independent and often fight.

When frightened, geese lower their heads, stretch out their necks, and flap their wings, honking and hissing loudly. Be careful you don't provoke a goose or you may get a nasty nip.

What a splendid display!

This turkey cock spreads out his tail feathers in a fan to attract a turkey hen. He drops his wing feathers down, puffs up the fleshy red dewbill that hangs above his beak and gobbles.

Turkeys are the largest birds found in the farmyard. They are traditionally eaten at Christmas in many parts of Europe or at Thanksgiving in the United States.

Turkeys were first brought to Europe by the Spaniards who discovered them in America over 400 years ago.

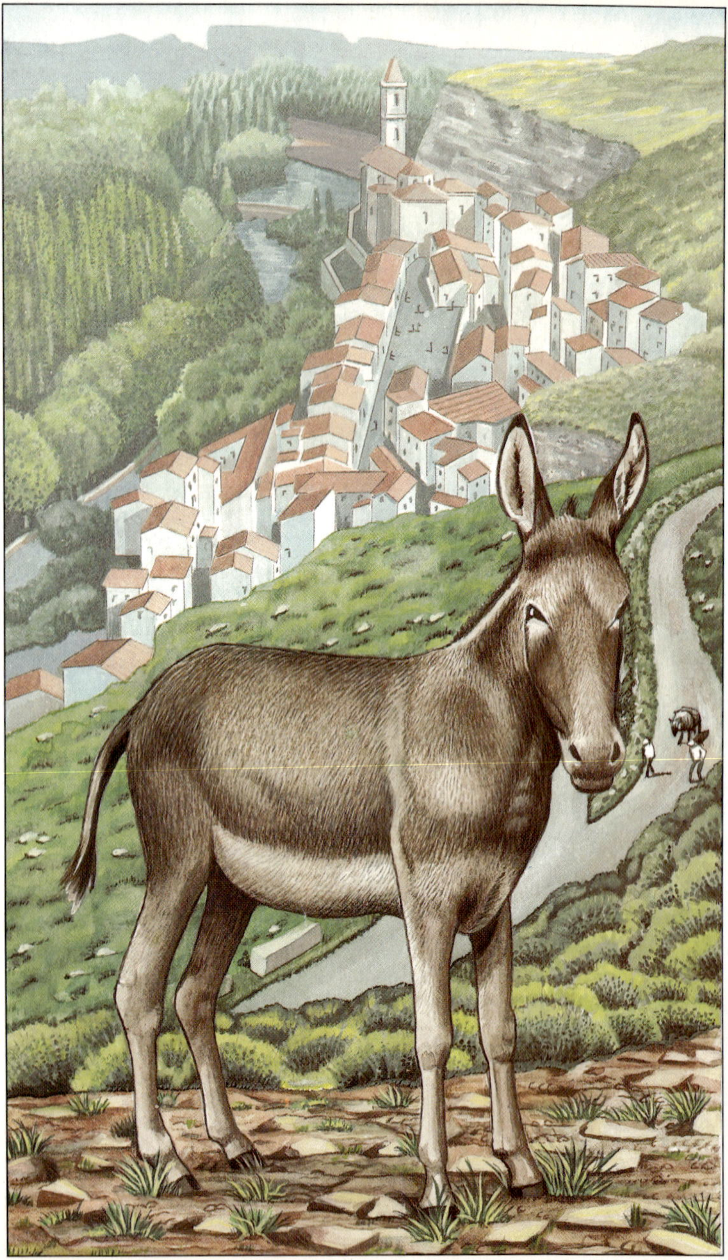

When you won't listen, has anyone ever said you are 'as stubborn as a mule'? Donkeys and mules sometimes do stop suddenly and refuse to budge!

Donkeys can pull very heavy carts.

In Mediterranean countries, like Greece or Spain, the donkey is used to carry heavy loads. All day long, under the burning sun, donkeys can clamber up the steepest and stoniest paths. They are very hardy but they need fresh water and time to graze. Both the mule and the hinny are cousins to the donkey.

A mule is a cross between a male donkey and a mare. A hinny is a cross between a male pony and a female donkey.

Mule

Hinny

Goats will eat anything.
Brambles, shrubs, or weeds.
They will even climb up trees
to nibble at tender young
leaves and shoots!
Nanny-goats provide
up to 2 litres of milk a day
which can be made into cheeses.

Goats need to be securely fenced in
as they can jump up to 1.5 metres high.
Don't go too near a goat: if she is angry
she may butt you with her horns.

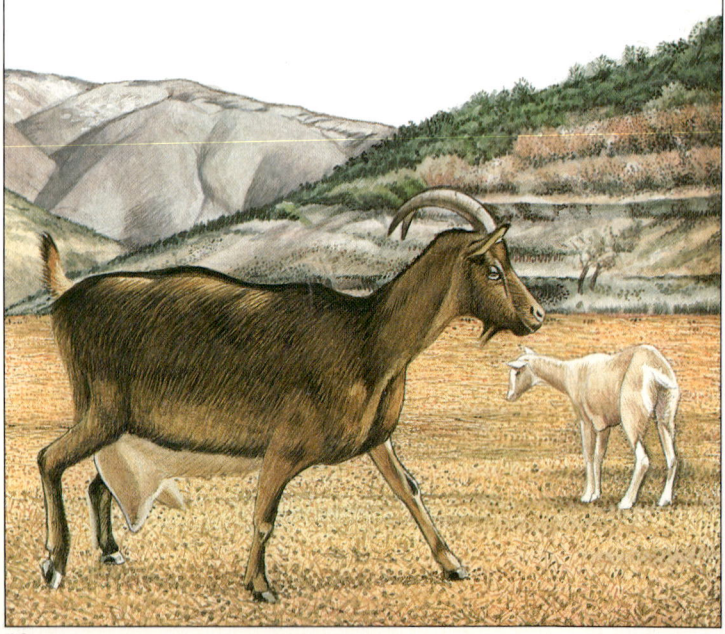

When sheep listen out for danger they prick up their ears.
If they are frightened, they scamper away with flattened ears.

Sheep are easily startled.

They follow each other everywhere, taking their lead from the head of the flock, usually the oldest ewe.

When they graze, sheep all face in the same direction with their backs to the wind.

They crop the grass very short.

Sheep thrive in hilly areas as they eat tough grasses and even heather.

**In summertime,
cows live outdoors in herds.**

No-one can distract cows when they are grazing! Heads lowered, tail and ears swishing to keep away the flies, cows walk about 4 km each day, eating around 60 kilos of grass as they go.

A cow does not give milk until she has her first calf at about two years old. Then she produces up to 20 litres of milk a day.

Pigs enjoy rolling in mud.
This is not because they are dirty
but to keep themselves cool.
With the tips of their snouts, they grub up
roots, worms and snails to eat.
Pigs eat almost anything and so they
are called omnivores.
They grow fat very quickly; at a year old
they may weigh between 100 and 150 kilos!

Many pigs today are
reared indoors in piggeries
and are not allowed out to forage.

Ducklings hatch out of their shells after 26 days.
They can swim and find their own food almost immediately.

The farmer has to help young turkey chicks dip their beaks in the feeding trough.

A doe or female rabbit can have up to 7 litters a year. She makes a soft nest for her babies with fur plucked from her underbelly.

Foals stand on their wobbly feet shortly after they are born. When they graze, they splay out their long legs to reach the grass!

A sow usually has twelve teats. The brightest piglets always choose one of the top ones which give the most milk.

The calf wraps its tongue round one of the cow's teats and sucks hard. A calf can drink about 10 litres of milk a day.

Farmers live in houses made of dried mud in some parts of Africa. Their animals run about freely.

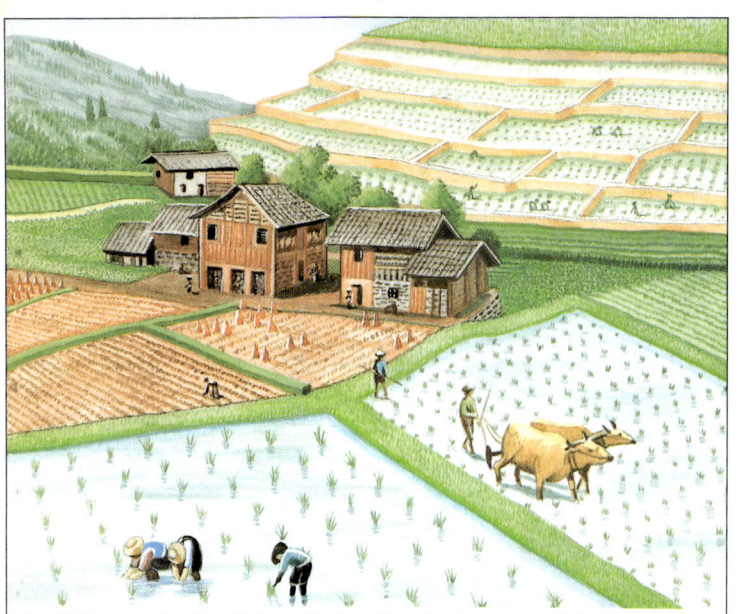

In China, water buffalo pull the ploughs in the paddy fields. Farmers also raise pigs, geese and ducks.

In the high plains of South America, farmers rear llamas.
Did you know that llamas spit if they are annoyed?

Farmers have to grow a lot of grain to feed their cattle in North America. They store it in tall silos.

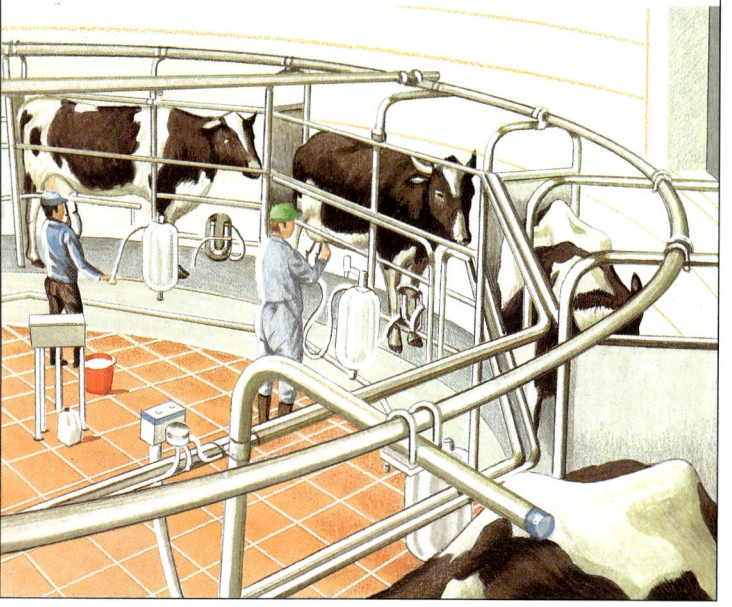

Farmers have to work very hard to feed their animals.

In spring, the farmer first ploughs the land with his tractor, turning over the earth.
Any big lumps are broken up with a harrow.
He then sows the seeds; wheat, oats or maize and plants potatoes or beets.
You may also see fields of bright yellow rape in flower. Most of the crops will be grown for animal feed.
Now is the time for the cows to go out into the meadows and the newly-shorn sheep to be sent into the hills.

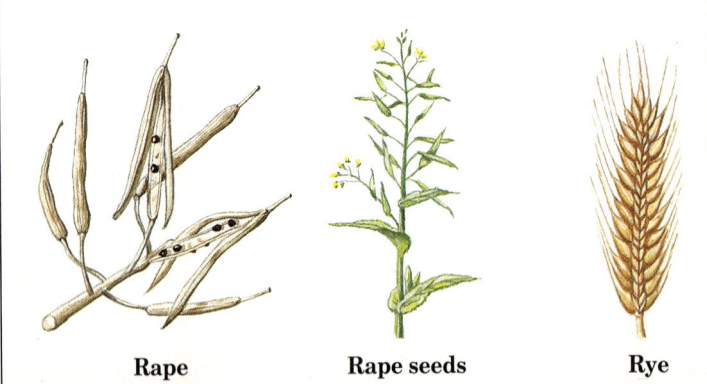

Rape   **Rape seeds**   **Rye**

Oats **Maize** **Spring rape**

In summer, the sun makes the grass grow
and ripens the grain.
The farmer hasn't a minute to spare.
He mows the dry grass for hay to feed
the animals in winter. He harvests
the wheat with a giant machine called
a combine-harvester and gathers up
the bales of straw to stack in the barns.
If a storm threatens, he works even faster
to get everything in before it rains.
Morning and evening the cows are milked.
They moo loudly if they are kept waiting!

In the autumn, the daylight hours are getting shorter, but there is still plenty to do. The last beets must be pulled from the ground, and the maize cobs laid out to dry in heaps or stacked in grain stores beside the fields.

Before digging the land again, the farmer spreads on fertilizer or manure. He sows the empty fields with winter wheat or rape and plants cabbages which can grow in the cold weather.

While they are inside in winter, cows eat lots of kale which looks like a large cabbage and is full of vitamins.

In winter, the ground may be frozen, but the farmer is kept busy looking after all his animals indoors! Animals need extra food as they cannot go out to find their own. At fixed times of day, the farmer brings them ground maize, beets and other fodder. He also has to change their bedding frequently.

At this time, the vet visits to check that all is well with the animals. He examines each one, vaccinating them against illness or perhaps helping a cow to give birth to her calf. Calves grow quickly in the warmth of the cowshed.

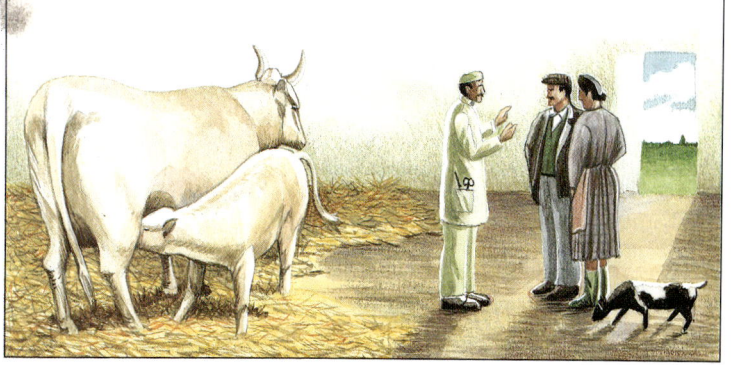

Some farms seem most unusual!

There are farmers who breed snails, snakes or even ladybirds by the thousand.

Snakes' venom is an important ingredient in making the vaccine for snakebites! Ladybirds are a useful pest control as they eat the greenfly which eat the crops. Mink and angora rabbits are kept commercially for their beautiful soft fur, although some people think that it is unkind to use these animals to make luxury fur coats.

Coypus were once reared for their warm fur. They look rather like small beavers.

Fish is very good for you and fish farming is now an important industry. Salmon and trout fisheries are the most common. The fish are kept in large tanks or cages which are put into lakes, rivers or the sea.

In South Africa, there are even ostrich farms.

Farm animal expressions!

When someone 'talks the hind-leg off a donkey' they talk non-stop.

If you 'put the cart before the horse' you switch the proper order of things.

To tell someone to 'hold their horses' means telling them to wait a moment.

'Getting someone's goat' means you are irritating or annoying them.

When a person 'rabbits on' they go on and on about the same subject.

If something is 'scarce as hen's teeth' it is very rare. If you 'chicken out' of something, you refuse to do it because you are scared.

A 'wolf in sheep's clothing' is someone who appears to be nice and gentle but is really sly and cunning.

Each farm animal has its own cry. Do you know them all?

Cows low, moo or bellow. Horses neigh or whinny. Sheep and goats bleat. Donkeys bray; you can hear the sound from far away! Pigs grunt, snort or snuffle. Rabbits are almost silent but squeak or squeal if frightened.

Geese honk and hiss. Turkeys gobble. Ducks quack when they waddle about. Chickens cluck and cackle, but the cock crows cock-a-doodle-doo to wake everyone up.

Try crowing like a cock in different languages:

The French say cocorico!
The Germans say kikeriki!
The Swedes say kuckeliku!
The Italians say chicchirichi!

Index

Africa, 24
America, North, 27
America, South, 26
animal behaviour, 10-21
animal eating habits, 14, 17-21, 31
animal fodder, 28-31
animal expressions, 13, 17, 34
animal sounds, 10, 35
aurochs, 7
baby animals, 22-23
beets, 28, 30
cattle, 7, 9, 20, 23, 27-29, 31, 35
chickens, 8, 10-13, 35

China, 25
combine-harvester, 29
coypus, 32
cross-breeding, 7
dewbill, 15
donkeys, 16-17, 35
ducks, 8, 11, 14, 22, 25, 35
egg-laying, 13
farm buildings, 9
farms around the world, 24-27
farmyards, 8-11
fertilizer, 30
fish farming, 33
foals, 23
fur farming, 32

geese, 10, 14, 25, 35
goats, 18, 35
grain, 27, 29
grazing, 19-20
guinea fowl, 10, 14
harvesting, 29-30
hinny, 17
kale, 31
ladybirds, 32
llamas, 26
maize, 28-30
milk production, 20, 23, 29
mink, 32
mules, 17
omnivores, 21
ostrich farming, 33

rabbits, 8, 22, 32, 35
rape, 28-30
pigs, 7-8, 21, 23, 25, 35
prehistoric times, 7
rams, 9
seasons on the farm, 28-31
sheep, 7, 9, 19, 28, 35
silos, 27
snakes, 32
turkeys, 11, 15, 22, 35
unusual animals, 32-33
vaccinations, 31-32
vets, 31
water buffalo, 25
wild boar, 7

Pocket Worlds – building up into a child's first encyclopaedia:

The Natural World
The Air Around Us
The Sunshine Around Us
The Moon and Stars Around Us
Our Blue Planet
Coast and Seashore
Mountains of the World
Volcanoes of the World
Deserts and Jungles
Rocks and Stones
In the Hedgerow
The Life of the Tree
Woodland and Forest
The Pond
Fruits of the Earth

The Animal World
Prehistoric Animals
The Long Life and Gentle Ways
  of the Elephant
Big Bears and Little Bears
Big Cats and Little Cats
Farm Animals Around
  the World
Cows and Their Cousins
All About Pigs
The Horse
Monkeys and Apes
Crocodiles and Alligators
Whales, Dolphins and Seals
Wolf!
Bees, Ants and Termites

Caterpillars, Butterflies
  and Moths
Birds and Their Nests
Wildlife Alert!
Wildlife in Towns
Animals in Winter
Animals on the Move
Animals Underground
Animal Architects
Animal Colours and Patterns
Teeth and Fangs

The World of Food
Chocolate, Tea and Coffee
Bread Around the World
The Potato
The Story of a Grain of Rice
Milk
All About Salt
All About Sugar

The World We Use
All About Wool
The Wonderful Story of Silk
The Story of Paper
What is Glass?
From Oil to Plastic
Metals and Their Secrets
Energy

The Human World
Living in Ancient Egypt
Living in Ancient Greece